ROOM IN MY HEART

I Have a Stepmom

By Amy Aalto

Illustrations by Stephen Adams and Victor Rigo

AuthorHouse™
1663 Liberty Drive
Bloomington, IN 47403
www.authorhouse.com
Phone: 1 (800) 839-8640

Published by AuthorHouse 12/09/2016

ISBN: 978-1-5049-1150-4 (sc)
ISBN: 978-1-5049-1151-1 (e)

Library of Congress Control Number: 2015907399

Print information available on the last page.

Any people depicted in stock imagery provided by Thinkstock are models,
and such images are being used for illustrative purposes only.
Certain stock imagery © Thinkstock.

This book is printed on acid-free paper.

Because of the dynamic nature of the Internet, any web addresses or links contained in this book may have changed
since publication and may no longer be valid. The views expressed in this work are solely those of the author and do not
necessarily reflect the views of the publisher, and the publisher hereby disclaims any responsibility for them.

authorHOUSE®

For Jeramiah

I have a Stepmom.

4

It took some time for us to get
to know each other, and for me
to decide what to call her.

Daddy and I decided on Mama-bear,
which felt comfortable to me, and
she calls me her Little-bear.

"I'm not little!" I tell her often. "I'm five

years old, and growing tall just like daddy!"

"Yes, you are growing tall", she will smile and say, "but you will *always* be my Little-bear."

At first, I wasn't so sure I wanted a Stepmom.

"I already have a mommy," I told daddy.

"Yes you do, and that will never change," he replied. "Now you also have a Stepmom who loves you, and is part of our family".

Mama-bear and I do many
things together.

We read, laugh, sing, bake cookies,
watch movies, buy groceries,
plant flowers, and even my *not*
so favorite thing to do...chores.

She also helps pick out my clothes,
and helps daddy tuck me in at night.

Daddy reminds me often that it is okay to accept Mama-bear's love. It doesn't mean I'm doing anything wrong or that I love anyone else any less.

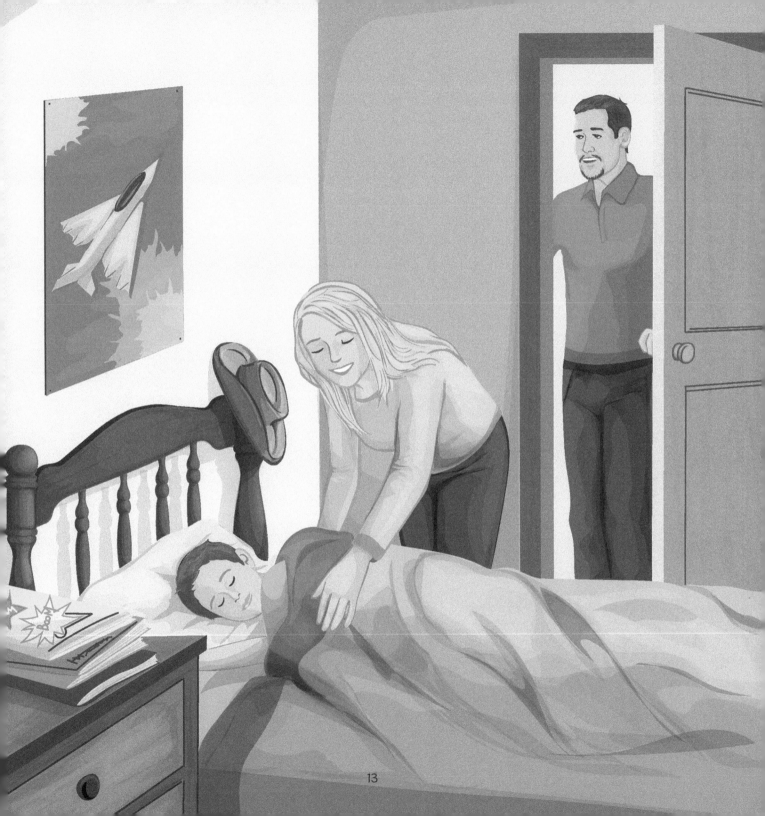

Once in a while, I feel really sad that my birth parents are divorced.

When I feel this way, I sometimes do not want to listen, eat my dinner, or be kind to Mama-bear.

When this happens, Mama-bear will try and make me smile by saying she is going to hug and s-q-u-e-e-z-e the grumpies out!

She means it too! She gives good hugs, and says that it is always okay to have sad feelings, but not to be unkind.

No matter what, I know that I am loved, and we are a family.

Daddy loves Mama-bear very much, and I love her too with all my might!

I know that it is okay to love my Birth Mom and my Stepmom.

There is plenty of room in my heart for them both!

9 781504 911504